Brilliant Brain Battles Bad Guys

Ellen Arnold

Illustrations by Deborah Farber

Zephyr Press®

Reaching Their Highest Potential

Tucson, Arizona

Acknowledgments

—To Tailor, whose creative energy powerfully shields us from bad guys—

Creating books takes work. But when you have a great team, the process can be joyful. Deborah Farber's picture-smart part helped develop my ideas into a wonderful visual presence. Marti Arnold's word- and number-smart parts were an invaluable asset in helping me be clear, concise, and consistent. Mary Temple's people-smart part provided me with constructive feedback on how to make this book a more powerful tool in helping young children deal with fears. Without their patience, ideas, and support, this project would still be in my mind rather than in your hands.

Brilliant Brain Battles Bad Guys

Grades K–4

Printed in the United States of America

ISBN 1-56976-111-6

Editor: Bonnie Lewis
Design & Production: Daniel Miedaner
Cover Design: Daniel Miedaner
Illustrations: Deborah Farber

Published by
Zephyr Press
P.O. Box 66006
Tucson, Arizona 87528-6006
http://zephyrpress.com
http://giftsforteachers.com

Library of Congress Cataloging-in-Publication Data

Arnold, Ellen, 1944-
Brilliant Brain battles bad guys / by Ellen Arnold ; illustrated by Deborah Farber.
p. cm.
ISBN 1-56976-111-6 (alk. paper)
1. Fear in children—Juvenile literature. [1. Fear. 2. Bullying. 3. Self-confidence.] I. Farber, Deborah, ill. II. Title.

BF723.f4 A78 2000
152.4'6—dc21 00-033398

Brilliant Brain Battles Bad Guys

A Note to Teachers and Parents:

It is a natural, normal developmental milestone when a child learns to control fears or imaginary threats. For students to be able to do this, they must first believe they have power over things in their minds. What better way to start than to battle the Bad Guys that are so often invading our thoughts? **MI Strategies for Kids,** a teacher/parent manual, describes a lesson plan that will help make this book a most useful tool for the learner.

Brilliant Brain's mind works in many ways. He likes to think about all kinds of things. But sometimes what he thinks about is Bad Guys. He doesn't always want to think about them, but sometimes he can't help it. Bad Guys just kind of appear in his head, sometimes when he is awake and sometimes when he is sleeping.

Sometimes Brilliant has fun pretending that Bad Guys are attacking someone else. Sometimes he feels powerful, pretending that he can get the Bad Guys to hurt someone he doesn't like. Sometimes Brilliant pretends that he can hurt the Bad Guys. But sometimes the Bad Guys get into Brilliant's imagination even when he doesn't want them there and doesn't want to play with them. Then, Brilliant thinks about how to get the scary Bad Guys out of his head.

And this is how he does it.

First, Brilliant thought about where the Bad Guys came from. He remembered when a big kid at school teased him. He remembered how afraid he felt if someone tried to pick a fight. He remembered how it felt to be called "stupid."

How have you tried to get rid of "bad guys" in your mind?

Each one of these memories added Bad Guys to Brilliant's brain. Brilliant didn't want to worry about these Bad Guys anymore. He didn't like them and he didn't want them to have any power over him. Still, he didn't know how to get rid of them.

Brilliant checked his strategy bank. He found strategies for listening, reading, skiing, and all kinds of things, but he couldn't find anything on how to help with his fear of the Bad Guys.

Brilliant decided to find his Smart Parts. So he put on his backpack and traveled down, around, across, and through Intelligence Avenue where the Smart Parts lived, to get some more strategies. He heard Music Smart strumming and humming.

BB: Music Smart, lend me your ear,
I need some help to deal with fear.
I have bad thoughts that won't go away,
Bad guys in my head that always say,
"Brilliant, we are going to get you."
Help me get rid of the fear I dread,
And tell Bad Guys to stay out of my head.
I get so scared; I don't know what to do.
I could really use a strategy or two.

MS: Hi there, Brilliant! I hear your song.
I have a tip to take along,
To help you feel more brave and strong.
Sing new words to the ABC song.
A, B, C, D,
You can't get me.
H, I, J, K,
I'll use a strategy.
Q, R, S,
You're not stronger than me,
W, X, Y, and Z.
Now I know how strong to be
So that you cannot scare me!
You can make sounds and
rhythms instead
To chase the Bad Guys from your head.

BB: I am strong. I have a voice. E, I, E, I, O.
And with my voice I can make a "roar," E, I, E, I, O.
With a roar, roar here and a roar, roar there,
Here a roar, there a roar, everywhere a roar, roar,
I am strong. I have a voice. E, I, E, I, O.
I am strong. I have a trombone. E, I, E, I, O.
And I can blow it all alone. E, I, E, I, O.
With a toot, toot here and a toot, toot there,
The Bad Guys, they all disappear!
I am strong. I have a trombone. E, I, E, I, O.

With all the singing and roaring, Brilliant stopped being scared. He got excited and kept adding more verses to his new song. He experimented with turning on the radio in his brain. He found out that he could change stations. He could change the volume, making his song louder or softer. He could tune in different kinds of sounds or instruments. This was fun. Using the magic radio in his brain, Brilliant didn't even think about being scared anymore.

Brilliant was using his "Sing a Song of Being Strong" strategy, which he put into his strategy bank backpack.

Brilliant continued looking around Intelligence Avenue until he spied Picture Smart.

BB: Picture Smart, I need to borrow your big eraser. I need to change a picture.

PS: What do you mean?

BB: I have a picture in my head and I don't want it there anymore. It is of the Bad Guys. I don't want to see it, but it seems to be there all the time. How do I get rid of it?

PS: I wouldn't get rid of it totally, Brilliant. And my eraser won't work in your head. That picture is there for a reason. Maybe it is there to protect you or remind you of something. But I know how to change the picture so it won't be scary anymore.

BB: How?

PS: You can change the size of the picture you see. Is it really big now? Then make it really, really tiny. Change the color. Does the picture in your mind have lots of bright colors? Then make them dingy and faded. Or if the colors are already dark, make them light and shiny. Is your picture dark and scary looking? Then adjust the light controls on the TV set in your brain and make it really, really bright. By changing these qualities of your picture, you can change how the picture affects you.

Brilliant turned on the special camera inside his brain. He thought about what Picture Smart had said. He looked at the Bad Guys in his head and changed the color and the brightness and the size. He added things. Pretty soon, the Bad Guys looked very silly. Brilliant laughed.

Then Brilliant sorted through the pictures his picture-smart part had taken that day. He saw what he had eaten for breakfast. He made the crust from his toast into a sword. He made his milk into a special formula for growing strong. He made the banana into a magic car that could sweep him away to a secret place. He imagined all the things on the table and how he could use them to chase away the Bad Guys.

His new picture was very powerful. And he was feeling powerful too.

Then he saw a picture in his head of one of the Bad Guys, Bad Brad. Brilliant felt his tummy get tight and his hands start to sweat. He was scared. But he remembered what Picture Smart had said. He concentrated really hard on the picture of powerful Bad Brad. Bad Brad carried a shield, to protect himself. Brilliant focused on the shield. He made it bigger. It changed from cardboard into metal. It began to grow. Letters began to appear on the shield. There was a **B**. *That could*

be for Brad. Then an **r**. *But the next letter wasn't an* a. *It was an* **i**. *Then more letters appeared in big, bright letters on the shield:* **l-l-i-a-n-t**. *It was his name. The shield flew from Brad's arm to Brilliant's. It looked great. Brilliant smiled. He felt very brave and powerful.*

PS: What is it, Brilliant?

BB: Oh, Picture Smart. I am sorry. I was looking at my picture. I did what you said. I took the picture of Bad Brad and changed it. Now I have the wonderful shield, and I feel so powerful.

PS: Did Brad scare you, Brilliant?

BB: No way. Not after the shield became mine. I felt strong and powerful, like no one could hurt me.

PS: Then I guess my "Powerful Pictures" strategy worked.

BB: It sure did. Thanks, Picture Smart.

What pictures would make you feel happy and strong, not scared?

Brilliant jogged over a bridge on Intelligence Avenue until he ran into Body Smart.

BB: Your toolbox looks really heavy, Body Smart.

BS: Hi, Brilliant. It would be heavy if I didn't work out all the time, but because I am so strong, it seems light to me. What can I do for you?

BB: Well, I need some new strategies. I'd like to find a way to battle the Bad Guys using my body smart part. If I work out and get muscles like yours, maybe I could just punch them and scare them away.

BS: Brilliant, fighting is one strategy but it rarely works, and you might get hurt. I'd rather teach you some other strategies. Besides, how would you punch the Bad Guys in your head?

BB: True. So what could I do?

BS: Pretend that you are a spider. Think about what it would be like. You could climb on anything. You could hide under the furniture. You could watch people when they didn't know you were watching. You could have lots of power as a spider. Try it.

Brilliant took Body Smart's advice. He got down on the floor and started to wiggle and squiggle his arms and legs in order to move. He pretended he had as many legs as a spider. Brilliant straightened each leg, one at a time. He moved quietly across the floor to the wall. He could feel each leg getting stronger and stronger as he pulled himself across the wall. He pretended to make a strong spiderweb as he moved, weaving the strands of the web so that no Bad Guys could get through. As soon as his web was big enough, Brilliant carried it above the imaginary Bad Guys and dropped it. The Bad Guys were trapped and could not get out.

Brilliant laughed and felt so proud of himself because he had used his "Be Strong and Powerful" strategy. This was certainly a strategy he wanted to keep. So he thanked Body Smart and put the strategy in his backpack. Brilliant meandered across a bridge and was looking at his reflection in the pond when he heard Self Smart quietly approach.

BB: Hi, Self Smart. I was just thinking. What do you think about Bad Guys?

SS: I don't like them. They make me feel uncomfortable.

BB: I need to do some thinking about Bad Guys. They have been troubling me, and I don't understand them. Some of them live inside my head, and I can't seem to get them to leave. Why do we have Bad Guys? Why do Bad Guys do things to people?

SS: Those are serious questions and ones I can't answer. You need to think about those questions for yourself. But I can tell you what I think. Sometimes the things I think about don't feel very good. But I can learn a lot from the thinking.

BB: I was thinking about what it would feel like if I were a Bad Guy. I don't think I would like it. I don't want people to hate me. It doesn't feel good. Do Bad Guys want to be hated? Do I become a Bad Guy when I get angry or jealous? I want to feel loved and loving instead.

SS: Feeling love is a great strategy. I look for a happy thought or feeling to balance the negative ones I have. That way, thinking doesn't make me feel sad. So find a happy thought in your head, Brilliant.

Brilliant looked inside his head for a happy thought. He remembered how happy he felt when his dad read to him or when he scored a goal in soccer. He liked thinking about how much fun it was to help his mommy cook, or help his sister learn to play pretend. He loved the feeling he got when he could tie his shoes all by himself.

Thinking about all these happy thoughts, Brilliant felt really good about himself. He felt important and able. Brilliant forgot all about the Bad Guys. They just went away.

Brilliant controlled his feelings through positive thoughts. He was using his "Feel Good" strategy.

BB: Thanks, Self Smart. You have helped me a lot with this strategy. I'll definitely put it in my backpack.

Brilliant walked through the woods surrounding Intelligence Avenue. All of a sudden, it got very dark and the wind started to howl. Brilliant thought he saw a Bad Guy hiding behind a tree. The wind picked up leaves and branches and threw them in the air. The rain came down so hard, it felt like a Bad Guy was shooting arrows at Brilliant's skin. Brilliant was cold and scared. He wished he were somewhere safe.

NS: Brilliant, hello there. What are you doing out in this storm?

BB: Oh, Nature Smart, I am so glad it is you. I was getting scared.

NS: Storms can be scary and dangerous, but they always have a purpose.

BB: But the howling wind sounded like a Bad Guy yelling at me. The blowing leaves and the strong raindrops made me feel like a Bad Guy was attacking me. I have been having a lot of trouble getting Bad Guys out of my head, and the storm just made it worse. Do you know a strategy I could try?

NS: Sure. I sometimes worry about Bad Guys harming the environment. And I get scared that Bad Guys will pollute the streams or cut down all the woods. So I try to keep calm with the "Everything Has a Reason" strategy.

BB: What's that?

NS: Come on under this bridge so you are out of the rain, Brilliant. You see, every time nature provides us with a challenge or problem, it also gives us something positive or beautiful. Like this storm. It is blowing and raining and not very pleasant outside, but when it is over, we will have enough rain for the plants to grow. And maybe we will even get a beautiful rainbow.

BB: How can that help me with Bad Guys?

NS: Even Bad Guys might have a positive side, once you get to know them. They have to let out their anger just like the wind, but if you are patient and try to understand how the Bad Guy works, you might find the rainbow in the Bad Guy. And if you understand the Bad Guy, he probably won't be so scary anymore.

Can you think of some-one or something that some people think is bad and you think is good?

BB: I don't think the Bad Guys have a rainbow.

NS: Well, think about our friend, Worldly Wolf. Is he a Bad Guy?

BB: No, Worldly Wolf is great fun. I love to play with him.

NS: What about the Rolling River right here? Is she a Bad Guy?

BB: No way, Rolling River is fun to swim in and fish in. I love hearing the sound of Rolling River as she runs down the hill. Today she is really loud, making a "whooshing" sound.

NS: But some people think wolves are mean and hurtful to people. And some people are very angry at Rolling River. Remember last summer, when we had so much rain? Rolling River was so full that she couldn't control all the water. Rolling River didn't stay in her own space. Instead, she overflowed and flooded many houses. It was a long time before Rolling River returned to her banks. Those people don't like Rolling River anymore. So you think of Rolling River and Worldly Wolf as your friends, but others think about them as Bad Guys.

BB: I never thought about it that way before. But I understand Worldly Wolf and Rolling River act differently sometimes because of things they can't control. Like Rolling River can't control the amount of rain that falls. And Worldly Wolf can't control how other people feel. And they don't mean to be bad. And if they do something, there is always a reason.

NS: Yes, in nature, you always have to think how things are connected. What are the reasons? What good will happen because of this? Like the strong wind warns us of a storm, or a clap of thunder warns us to get shelter from the rain. And then after the storm there is a rainbow. Like now, look, Brilliant. The storm is over and there is a rainbow in the sky.

BB: Wow. I need to think about this some more. I think I'll just sit here by Rolling River and think. Thanks, Nature Smart, for the "Everything Has a Reason" strategy.

After the sky cleared and Brilliant had time to think about the new strategies he had collected, he meandered back along Intelligence Avenue until he saw someone reading.

WS: Brilliant, would you like to read with me?

BB: Hi, Word Smart. What are you reading?

WS: A chapter book. It is really a good one, about letters and how they fit together to make words.

BB: Could you find a book that deals with scary Bad Guys? I need some strategies to deal with Bad Guys and how to get them out of my head.

WS: I am sure I have heard your mother tell you "Brilliant, don't hit. Use your words." Words can be much stronger than fighting. They really can help you get what you want.

BB: But words don't scare the Bad Guys away. If I said nicely, "Please go away," the Bad Guy would just keep teasing and hiding and scaring me.

WS: Then use words that Bad Guys don't care for, words that are funny or silly, not scary. I'll help if you want. Let's use the letters from ***Bad Guy*** and spell out some good words.

So Brilliant took all the letters in **B-A-D G-U-Y** *and found words to go with each one. They had to be words that were funny or happy. That way the Bad Guy wouldn't like them.*

B could be for *battle* or *boxing,* but those are words the Bad Guy likes. Instead, Brilliant thought about *beautiful bananas* and *bouncing balls* and *baskets of bagels* and *blowing bubbles.*

A could be for *anger* and *aggression,* but those are words the Bad Guy would like. Instead, Brilliant thought about *artichokes in applesauce* and *ants arriving* and *asking advice from ABBA.*

D could be for *danger* and *dungeons,* but those words are ones the Bad Guy would like. So Brilliant thought of fun words like *dancing dogs* and *dramatic Dylan* and *darling dragonfly dolls.*

G could be for *gigantic* and *grouchy gorilla,* words the Bad Guy would like. But Brilliant decided to use the words *giggling girls* and *glorious green galoshes* and *gentle Ginger.*

U could be for *ugly* and *unfriendly.* But instead, Brilliant used *upside down uniforms* and *Uncle Cass* and *Uncle Russ under umbrellas in their underwear.*

Y could be for *yucky* and *yelling.* But instead, Brilliant thought about *yellow, yummy yams,* and *young yaks yodeling.*

Brilliant laughed at some of his positive and funny word combinations.

BB: Thanks, Word Smart. I feel better already, using your "Positive Words" strategy to battle the Bad Guys. I will add the "Positive Words" strategy to my strategy bank.

Brilliant strolled down the path and jumped over the stepping stones on Intelligence Avenue, thinking about the best way to solve his problem. Now he had several choices, but which one would work best? Each time he added another strategy to his backpack, he felt better. But he still wasn't sure which strategy would be best for him.

BB: Number Smart, do you have an answer for me?

NS: Well, I need to know the problem before I can come up with a solution.

BB: I need more strategies, this time to battle the Bad Guys. They seem to live in my brain all the time, and I want to get rid of them.

NS: Is there any pattern to when the Bad Guys come out? How many times a day do the Bad Guys try to play? How many friends do the Bad Guys have? How old are the Bad Guys? How did the Bad Guys get stronger? Are the Bad Guys always Bad Guys? How many other ways do Bad Guys act? How much food do the Bad Guys eat in a day? How high could the Bad Guys count? Could you count as high? How high could you count if you did it together?

BB: Wow, Number Smart. You sure have a lot of questions. I don't know the answers to any of them!

NS: You don't know them now, but you could. Just start keeping track of what you know and finding the answers to what you don't know.

BB: I think it would be fun to work on all these questions, trying to figure out how much or what time or doing comparisons.

NS: You probably won't be worried about the Bad Guy anymore, if you are so busy with all these questions.

BB: But I have other questions I use. How do you solve a math problem? How do you know if you have it right? Is there a way to figure it out? Can you add something to both sides or can you make things equal?

NS: Now let's see if you can use these questions for your Bad Guys. How do you start to solve the Bad Guy problem?

BB: You think of what you know and what is unknown.

NS: How do you know if you have it solved?

BB: Well, I won't think about the Bad Guys all the time.

NS: Is there a way to figure out the Bad Guys?

BB: I guess I have been getting great ideas from all the Smart Parts.

NS: Can you add something to both sides to make things equal?

BB: Well, if I gave both me and the Bad Guys smiles and laughter, then we would be equal. Or I can give both sides songs, or both sides silly words, or . . .

NS: I think you have it figured out now, Brilliant.

BB: Thanks, Number Smart. I guess the "Question It" strategy could work for dealing with Bad Guys.

Brilliant was worried that if he had to play alone, he might see a Bad Guy. So he wandered back down Intelligence Avenue and found People Smart talking to friends.

PS: How are you today Brilliant?

BB: Not so good. I have been scared of the Bad Guys in my head, and I am collecting strategies to battle them.

PS: We have an idea. Let us introduce you to a friend who knows all about Bad Guys.

Brilliant saw a soft stuffed snake named Squiggles, on the ground next to People Smart. He started talking to Squiggles. Squiggles' raspy voice sounded strange.

BB: Squiggles, can you make the SSSSS sound? Is it hard or easy for you?

Squiggles flickered his long tongue and made a long hissing sound. "SSSSSSSSS."

Brilliant and Squiggles talked and laughed. Brilliant asked Squiggles about Bad Guys.

BB: Why are so many people afraid of snakes?

Squiggles: Prejudice. Some people hear something bad about a snake, and then they assume that I am bad, even though they don't know me. I try to be sensitive to that. I show them that I am really nice and they don't have to be afraid of me. But I have to take it slow. I can't rush up to them because then I scare them. I watch, listen, and then slowly approach them. Sometimes I do nice things for them, and then they learn to trust me. But I can't blame them for being scared. It isn't their fault. They just don't know that snakes can be nice. So I have to teach them.

Brilliant thought about using Squiggles' ideas. Was he prejudiced against Bad Guys? Were some Bad Guys nice, like Squiggles? Brilliant decided he would use the "Don't Be Prejudiced" strategy.

Brilliant reviewed the strategies he got from each of the Smart Parts, so that he could battle the Bad Guys.

BB: Music Smart gave me the "Sing a Song of Being Strong" strategy. When I sing this song I feel better and it chases the Bad Guys away.

BB: Picture Smart drew me the "Powerful Picture" strategy. By changing the size and shape of the picture, I ended up having a wonderful shield that could protect me and help me feel powerful.

BB: Body Smart helped me become a spider with a magic web. This was the "Be Strong and Powerful" strategy.

BB: Self Smart wanted me to think about the "Feel Good" strategy. I searched in my head for a thought that helped me feel good instead of being scared.

BB: Nature Smart helped me understand the "Everything Has a Reason" strategy so I can think about how different people interpret the same thing in different ways. I can try to see if there is a purpose or a reason for things that I find scary.

BB: The "Positive Word" strategy came from Word Smart. We made up funny and positive words to go with the letters *in BAD GUY.* Some of those words made me laugh.

BB: Number Smart added the "Question It" strategy, where I had to come up with all kinds of questions, like I do for math, and use them to think about the things that are scaring me.

BB: People Smart is always making friends and gave me the "Don't Be Prejudiced" strategy. Squiggles taught me how to think about whether I am scared for a good reason, or because I have pre-judged someone based on what I have heard from others.

So, remember, when you feel scared, you can use all your smart parts to battle the Bad Guys in your world.

And when you do, you will be just as smart as Brilliant.